Audrey Ardern-Jones

Doing the Rounds

Indigo Dreams Publishing

First Edition: Doing the Rounds
First published in Great Britain in 2019 by:
Indigo Dreams Publishing
24, Forest Houses
Cookworthy Moor
Halwill
Beaworthy
Devon
EX21 5UU

www.indigodreams.co.uk

Audrey Ardern-Jones has asserted her right under the
Copyright, Designs and Patents Act 1988 to be identified as the
author of this work.
© Audrey Ardern-Jones 2019

ISBN 978-1-912876-15-0

British Library Cataloguing in Publication Data. A CIP record
for this book can be obtained from the British Library.

Designed and typeset in Palatino Linotype by Indigo Dreams.
Cover painting by Audrey Ardern-Jones.
Printed and bound in Great Britain by 4edge Ltd.

Papers used by Indigo Dreams are recyclable products made
from wood grown in sustainable forests following the guidance
of the Forest Stewardship Council.

For My Family

CONTENTS

Doing the Rounds

Doing the Rounds

Agnieszka was muttering in Polish
scattering crusts for city sparrows
when kids on bikes lunged at her
went for the unzipped bag

coins, holy cards, medals lay
loose on cracked slabs
beads of a broken wooden rosary
strewn deep in the gutter

as she lay on the pavement
she thought back to her homeland
a child rounded up
trudging with the thousands

on cobbled roads, unmade tracks
holding her father's hand
bodies in the snow, Russian soldiers
in grey woollen overcoats

burning the ice with guns
all this she told me, on the ward
knowing my mother, like her
escaped Lwów, kept going

White Roses
(for my mother)

She never spoke about her early life in Lwów,
she told me about ECT to numb the pain,
how she left at midnight, a last minute tip-off,
escaping under sheets in pelting ice-cold rain.

She told me about ECT to numb the pain,
she left without giving a kiss to her mother,
escaping under sheets in pelting ice-cold rain,
fearful about the fate of her missing brother.

She left without giving a kiss to her mother,
rushed outside by her father, no time to pack,
fearful about the fate of her missing brother,
a young trainee doctor who never came back.

Rushed outside by her father, no time to pack,
she fled a flowerless city where thousands died,
a young trainee doctor who never came back,
she said a rosary at night, lit a candle and cried.

She fled a flowerless city where thousands died,
she'd high cheek bones, blue eyes, blonde hair,
she said a rosary at night, lit a candle and cried,
no mementos of her family to help the despair.

She'd high cheekbones, blue eyes, blonde hair,
she said a rosary at night, lit a candle and cried,
no mementos of her family to help the despair,
she never spoke about her early life in Lwów.

Night Terrors

So many midnights dreaming of spiders –
my mother under an African mesh-mosquito net,
my parents' bed a hide-away from creatures
in the dark crossing my red-tiled floor, the winged
insects buzzing up my walls.

I'd snuggle in my mother's side of the bed,
careful not to hurt her TB twisted hand, a pale zip-line
scarred on her left forearm – she'd hug me tight
like the rolled up white sheet she carried
fleeing through the Carpathian mountains.

She'd cry in her sleep *Pomóż mi! Pomóż mi!*
a staccato of jerks – the enemy somewhere near.
Her Pond's cold cream dissolving, my feet asleep across
her tummy – I'd dream of playing dragon-shadows
on sunlit walls, lizards hiding in the cracks.

Pomóż mi – help me (Polish)

Penn Hill

Faceless faces of 1930 pebbledash houses line up the avenue
on Penn Hill. Ladies in plastic macs and floral headscarves

gossip outside the post-office about who's died, and what
the Doctor said last week. Inside Mrs Jenkins sits behind

a grill counter-top taking in parcels. I pay mother's bills:
the papers, packets of Player's, stamps and airletter cards.

In the greengrocer's shop Nora uses ancient see-saw scales
to weigh turnips, carrots & potatoes in brown paper bags.

Only the pink-faced chemist wearing metal specs and a white
coat knows my name. I hand him mother's prescriptions,

Mogadon, Valium – I see him pouring pills into a glass bottle.
I wait, safe in this crushed shop hidden by shelves of soaps,

hot water-bottles, eau de colognes, pink hairnets and flannels.
For my sake, he adds in cod liver oil, plus a pot of malt.

He asks after mother, I tell him she cries most nights. On
Sundays she takes us to Mass, lights a candle to Our Lady

of Sorrows, counts the days when she'll be with Daddy again
in Africa, leaving us behind, our name tapes sewn safely on.

Only Ten More Months

On Sundays after Mass, we write letters home
with fountain pens in Italic script, navy-blue ink.
Sister James sits in charge of our classroom,
red face like a red traffic light under a black veil.

She marks our homework in the sniggering hush.
Girls write about best friends and worst friends
and convent food – cold rice pudding and gravy
stew with hardly any meat but lumps of spuds.

Outside an autumn bonfire fogs up our windows,
the rust-brown scent of smoke takes me home
to the bush fires burning, yellow tufts of grass
in clearings near stumps of armless charcoal trees.

I try hard not to cry as I lick down the edges of my
blue airmail letter card – it's October, we'll be home
in July. I think of the flight stops we make en route:
Paris, Athens, Nairobi, Entebbe and lastly, Lusaka.

Playgrounds

Children yelp and shout on monkey-bars, slides,
swings and roundabouts; a chorus of *Higher!*
Higher! Watch me! Watch me!

The racket takes me back to my childhood,
the tyranny of tag – *Catch me! Catch me!*
Mid-morning breaks stuck outside in the cold,

eating white bread spread with dripping,
poking straws through half-pint glass bottles,
slurping milk under the frozen cream.

In the chilblain air we play hopscotch and jacks
on concrete until Sister Anthony blows her whistle,
her face ballooning like a frog in a wimple.

No-one dares to talk. At noon, the Angelus bell
rings in threes. In the courtyard, nuns gather
to pray in silence – *Angelus Domini nuntiavit Mariae...*

Who's Afraid

Sister Imelda warned us about wolves,
said they lurk in dazzling outfits –
tight trousers and leather jackets – they
hide in bars and pubs and on the upper decks
of buses – I believed her for years, never
setting foot upstairs – footsteps lurking...

Nowadays, I always ride on the top of a bus
like a child on a merry-go-round.
I'm not missing out any more – knowing
wolves were once everywhere
waiting to eat me up – somehow, I don't think
I'm tasty enough these days.

The Tree We Left Behind

We hugged you, rode you like a horse,
swung upside down on your branches.

You were our nest in the summer holidays,
hiding us from the heat – from the beak

of an African hawk-eagle swooping low,
high notes in his voice warning us about

the *black mamba* slithering nearby, spitting
his inky arrows and flashing his eyes.

He never dared climb you. I think he knew
we were safe in your hollow, out of his reach.

These days, in the midst of any storm, I close
my eyes, breathe in the scent of your bark,

see the green-yellow light on your leaves,
taste the sweet juice of mangoes in the dark.

Lion in Chingola

strangers surround him
touch his lifeless paws; I hold my father's hand
watch the bare-chested men
wipe their rifles – expect his mouth to open
to roar, to eat me up

he lies centre stage in a bungalow lounge
no bones, no flesh, a mouth with no tongue
I stroke his quilt of beige-gold skin, *uli musuma*
tail-swipe my brother poking sixpences
through bullet holes

outside, men slash sun-burnt grass
inside my mother tries to sleep, curtains drawn
the air dense, another migraine

uli musuma – you are beautiful (Bemba)

Watching the Boys, My Freckles Burning

they made carts most days
out of dumped objects from mounds of rubbish:
spokes, fridge doors, disused frames
saddles of all shapes
a cracked dynamo connected
to broken handle bars
a flattened orange box hammered
to the back of an old radio threaded by wires
from wrecked Land Rovers

boys whistling, they'd push off
puffs of pumped air
rows of split inner tubes, ripped slits of light
cracking blackness, zings of endless bells
squeaks from squashed rubber-hooters
wheels running loose
from hills too steep, passing our house
on the way to the township
calling out *Nkonka! Nkonka!*

Nkonka – Follow me (Bemba)

In the Fifties

Mporokoso's villagers believed African stars
were the eyes of the dead, the spirits of others

unwilling to be born. That the moon was a man
who angered the sun, and that the sun in his fury

came down in the night and ignited the trees –
frantic animals rushing away from the *bundu*

racing towards the Ntumbachushi waterfalls,
where painted tribal chiefs in necklaces of bones

and beads soaked themselves in the cold Ng'ona
River – their blessings dipped under the water

away from the heat of the orange-smoked hems,
low flames wavering on the distant horizon.

And us, on a veranda, listening to golden voices
on the *World Service*, paraffin lamps, luminous

in black, mother smoking and drinking her gin,
father with an ice-cool beer, handing us cokes.

Mosquitoes buzzing as we scratched bites
on our faces, on sunburnt pink arms, legs – scorpions

switching colours under mango trees where
miombo tits pecked the mealy bugs. We were

the foreigners in darkness – it was hot then,
burning in ways I didn't know.

bundu – Bantu word for 'the wilds'

I'm Listening to Forecasts of Violent Winds

The fishermen are drawing in nets,
the shops have shut early,
the dog, he is whining, whining

and won't go out. I prop a garden seat
against the tilted shed, watch
bursts of beetles skitter across the lawn.

I track back to my African childhood –
matebele ants marching in lines hissing
over parched ground, men waiting

for dust-driven whirlwinds, witchdoctors
lambasting the sick for their sins, babies
strapped on backs, women running

and shouting in Bemba *Chili mupepi!*
Chili mupepi! The dry heat, the drum beat,
the wind that zipped inside itself and exploded.

Chili mupepi – It's Near (Bemba)

Names From Another Era

Softie helped mother in the house. He cared
for us as children, cared for us as teenagers.
He dressed in khaki, a tunic top with lots
of pockets. He'd no lines on his face. He taught us
Bemba, *mwapoleni mukwai*, how are you, *natolela sana*
thank you very much; a burnt umber voice settling
sibling quarrels – *shh* a finger over his mouth.

Macaroni wore white and a black tasselled hat
like a fez. Dimples, deep set eyes, a missing
finger on his right hand – he'd polish floors,
wash windows, clean the veranda and helped
prepare lunch or supper. He liked to chat
as he laid the table – asking us about the copper
named napkin rings, whose was whose.

Sixpence trimmed edges, pruned the roses,
petunias, cut back the pink-red bougainvillea
in the winter, dug ditches in the rainy season.
He liked to whistle tunes, mostly he wore a vest
over shorts, smoking and coughing as he worked.
He used to let us mess with the garden hose,
squirt water at each other, play *splash* in the heat.

These days place names have changed, my
sister's birthplace Abercorn is now Mbala.
Our home town Broken Hill is Kabwe, Bancroft
on the Copperbelt is Chililabombwe. Maybe,
people's names have changed too: Softe to Sonwe,
Macaroni to Mutohla, and Sixpence to Sililo.
Zambian names in perfect rhythm.

.

A Recent Visit to Lusaka

In the Soweto market on Lumumba road
trippers taste dried Kapenta fish and cured caterpillars.
Locals fry termites in pans and buy mopane worms.
On Saturdays, the football stadium is crowded,
fans rooting for Lusaka Dynamos.
At night, club music echoes full volume
over high-rise flats and lit-up sky-scrapers
under an African moon.

In the suburbs, untamed dogs bark in unnamed streets
where mud roads meet tarmac, where boys with scythes
cut grass near nail-netted boundaries.
Where barefoot men in the Kalingalinga compound
drink *kachasu*, cut their feet on the broken glass,
smoke roll-ups, swear in Nyanja,
and stumble back to makeshift homes,
mosquitoes sucking liquor from their lips.

I walk this place with Sister Ann,
tread down rubbish on the stone-pebble ground.
We visit a young boy, no tyres on his wheel-chair,
puffed legs, torn patches on his shorts.
He greets us with a grin – pools of darkness
fill his mother's eyes, a baby
strapped on her back, arms folded,
crumbs on the ground, ants everywhere.

A Place in My Heart: the Missionary Doctor in the Ward

he told me stories
about his life in Kiminini
as I gave him sips of water

he'd learned Swahili
to talk with villagers
to dispel fears of witch doctor's spells

drums in the dark
mothers weeping
at newborn's screams

he operated most days
and in candle-light, tsetse flies swarming
the scent of nakedness

as he faded I held
his spindle hands in mine
hummed hymns

left over from my childhood
when he died
we closed his eyes

soap washed his bone-thin
golden body
dried and wrapped him

later that night I felt his presence
in my nurses room
he knew he was my first ever death

Ghazal

His mother says he's very poorly; he's in a darkened space,
his eyes are sore, he's feeling very sick, he's four years old.

She tells me the GP missed meningitis, said it was winter flu,
a bad headache and a high temperature, he's four years old.

She rang 999, he can't move his neck, he's a rash on his face,
on his legs – his hands and feet are ice, he's four years old.

She says his favourite story is about a tiger and tea. *Is it true?*
I ask him, *I'm terrified of tigers*, he giggles – he's four years old.

She reads his book, it's as though the tiger's in an eating race
finishing up the food & drink – he sits up, he's four years old.

She asks him to have a drink of water, holds up his cup, *No do.*
He shakes his head, pushes her hand away, he's four years old.

I'm struck by the way she puffs his hospital pillows into place,
the way she holds his teddy close to him, he's four years old.

Her pain filters through to me, I burn inside – I say he's due
his antibiotics. I pull a silly face, he laughs, he's four years old.

Daphne

This visit she told me she was sick
of care workers calling her *darling*,
fed up with the smell of lavender,
fed up with play-acting – an actress
who loved to lead trumps, finesse
with the Queen of Spades.

She said she needed to tell the truth,
break a privacy promise and talk
about her days in post-war Berlin,
her hidden world – cigarettes, jazz,
girls in bars, men in felt hats, cigars,
paper envelopes in coat pockets.

Pills left untouched on her locker,
warm air filled the room as she spoke,
her muffled voice spilling
her secrets, her eyes closing as she
drifted away. I removed her glasses –
they'd slipped sideways.

Award Winning Care Home

the night-nurse found him in bed with Elsie
he'd tipped flowers on the floor
drunk water from the vase, thought sheets were sand
the corridor a route to find the beach

they said he had a right
not to shut his door, not to have cot sides
a right to wander if he wanted – but he didn't know
his name, didn't know how to speak

at breakfast they found him
spilling cornflakes down his jumper
eating bacon with his fingers, drinking
tea backwards

days after he arrived, the Sister in charge
called his daughter, told her to search
for another home – her tone like a head teacher
expelling a child from school

Night Talk

He speaks of death – his death, how parts
of him have died. It's midnight,
he's on my computer screen, grey metal limbs
in trainers, no socks under green trousers.

He has half a right arm, a large left hand,
three rings on his little finger, a creased forehead,
a rounded mouth as he tells his story
about a snowball that saved his life:

one the hospice nurse brought to his bed,
made him catch, crunch, feel the chill,
one that made him laugh again –
the dust of snow in white-blue air.

Threads

She was twenty-eight when diagnosed, black
hair stolen by chemo, she wore a blonde wig

with a wispy fringe. She told me, she'd traced
her family history searching names on gravestones.

I listened to stories of forgotten people, how Nana
and her sister were diagnosed in their forties,

how Mammy died when she was nine and how
her brother was diagnosed last year at thirty four.

Memories of offered masses and sacred litanies,
her hands in mine, arms lighter than a doll's,

her face translucent as almond soap. I spoke
of what she knew, names of high-risk genes,

fate as dice, and that her sibling's and children's
chances were as at birth, 50/50 like a girl or boy.

She gave a blood sample for all the family,
knowing if an alteration in a gene were found,

her family could choose to have genetic testing,
knowing that choices are never easy, never sure.

For now, she prays to be well for her daughter
sitting beside her, eating crackers in a pushchair.

Left Ventricular Failure in the Early Hours

He said it was a nice funeral
     despite neighbours admiring wrong flowers
orange roses in a wreath on the ground
     he could only think of
how she used to make ginger marmalade
     around this time in January

Doctors
(for J & L)

She had always been afraid of needles,
scared of hospitals, and when her waters
broke, she thought she was drowning.

After the epidural and the safe delivery,
she told the anaesthetist Jason, she'd like
to name her son after him. Her hero of the day.

A few weeks later she rang the surgery
requesting a visit as the baby was crying,
wouldn't sleep, and she was desperate.

A lady doctor came, noticing the clusters
of white snowdrops in the morning freeze.
The baby slept as the GP examined him.

She listened to his heart, his lungs and looked
inside his ears. She said the baby was fine.
They talked flowers, and how they both loved

the sight of summer's marigolds. The sun shone
warming a mass of yellow jasmine petals,
a shower of stars melting the winter ice.

Bluebells

I feel the spikes of a hedgehog
under my hospital white cotton
sheets. I'm told it's my raised
temperature prickling my back.
I've a lavender bag hidden under
my pillow. The *shh shhing* gusts
of oxygen are soporific. I sleep
in waves and specify no visitors.
I dream of the delicate scents of
bluebells warmed by an afternoon
sun. They are not for picking.

I Speak for Nurses Worldwide

who in summer suns under burning skies
hold hands of the dying despite the sores

who in fog-grey mists of locked-up wards
talk gently to the confused, the paranoid

who unclip, clip, check and check again
the mystical noises of the hospital gadgets

who speak in soft sounding ocean voices
soothing the secrets of unconscious minds

who in the rush of busy early mornings
visit newborns and the homebound sick

who guard the cot sides of a fevered child
catching dragonflies by the garden pond

who tuck in safely an old lady, she thinks
she's picking buttercups on her sheet

I speak for nurses worldwide who honour
nurse heroines of their day, of any day.

Sixteen

I have often thought of Isabella,
a Down's syndrome daughter,
and her Mum, the day our girls

were born, our beds beside each other.
Shrill cries of newborns echoing
through the long ward.

Somehow, we never said goodbye,
though we promised some day
we'd meet up. We never did.

I'm sitting opposite my daughter,
she's wearing a second-hand Russian
coat she bought on a school trip.

We're going to Kings Cross station
to meet Marie-Clare, her French
exchange she doesn't like.

On the other side of the carriage,
I see Isabella with her mother, her eyes
brighter than a sky bird

with a smile that fills the sea – in the iced
silence of the train-travelling nobodies,
they're laughing.

The Lady on the Isle of Mull

she flicks salted bread
into a storm of Greylag geese
steers the corncrake-chicks
from the iris bed

across a path to strawberry fields
horses know her voice
as she cloaks them
in the freezing fog

she carries a whistle inside
her rucksack and herds up
escapees, lambs lost on tracks
leading to nowhere

a rescuer of upturned beetles
lost fledglings, she speaks to herself
as she spins pebbles across
the skin of an empty sea

at night she crochets octopuses
in brightly coloured wools
each tentacle shaped like
an umbilical cord

After Sacro Monte di Ossuccio

When I prepare a feast
of *cotoletta alla milanese* I have the heart of an Italian.
When I have the heart
of an Italian, a Madonna appears.
When a Madonna appears,
I tell her about my fears, the sound of bones under water.
When I tell her about the sounds of bones under water,
she finds beads deep in a lake.
When she finds beads deep in a lake,
she makes a rosary, threads it with gold from her hair.
When she makes a rosary,
threads it with gold from her hair, I bathe in shallow waters.
When I bathe in shallow waters, I find stars on split rocks
and minnows make veils of themselves over my shoulders.
When I find stars on split rocks
and minnows make veils of themselves over my shoulders,
I hear the bells of Santa Maria Assunta.
When I hear the bells of Santa Maria Assunta,
I light a candle in a rose-lit chapel in a lemon grove
of an empty monastery.
When I find an empty monastery, I discover a dining room
and prepare a feast of *cotoletta alla milanese.*

Caravelas
(for Fabricio & Lucas)

Somewhere, there's always a sky –
skies spilling rains over mountains,
tributaries filling rivers through
thousands of forests, fish dipping
deep under waters, endless surf
trailing white-gold sands – scorched
cacti under blue in the Sertão desert.

Somewhere, there's always an aroma,
cafés with Arabica percolated coffee,
aromas of ripening guavas, Tahiti
limes and coconuts – orange-bellied
sabiás pecking the fruit, sweet smelling
roses under the statue of Our Lady
of Aparecida, candles burning.

Somewhere, there's always music,
the Samba, the Forró, the Baião,
dancers dancing barefoot, the heat,
the flute – guitarists strumming, a singer
sings jazz, short skirts, red lipstick,
feet inside feet, hips inside hips, a fanned
hand like a star, flat on a naked back.

Somewhere, there's always a party,
cachaça, caipirinha, feasts of *salpicão*,
mandioca frita, creme de papaia,
brothers, sisters, cousins, second
cousins, uncles and aunties, children
playing at midnight, babies on laps,
outside, dogs barking, barking, barking…

Night Train through Uttar Pradesh

The carriages are full, families lie curled together
sleeping on bunks, blankets covering their heads.

The man in the bunk below me eats his curry from
a paper box – shares it with his wife and child.

I read with my torch before I sleep. The conductor
wakes us, checking and clipping our tickets. Outside,

we hear calls of the cockerels rousing the villagers,
a wash of peach-gold light spills over the rice fields.

We pass women in coloured saris, pink, gold, green
and sapphire blue – children wave at us, wave again.

I wave back, snap-flashing images with my camera,
a mother turns and glares at me. I delete my photos.

Her look stays inside me. The train trundles on to Delhi
where crowds meet us, push us across the platforms.

Outside the station, I'm swept over by a sea of children,
a sing-song of voices – *Take my picture! Take my picture!*

The Elephant of Madurai

We queue to meet him, he greets us, his trunk tickles our skirts,
he bends his knee, lowers his tusks, smiles with his eyes closed.

Today's a day for devotees' photo-shoots – bundles of rupees
for keepers Sanjay and Ravi – he strikes the perfect pose.

He's worshipped in this sacred place, at weddings he's adorned
with umbrellas of peacock feathers and jewelled gold throws.

At night a trumpet sounds in the temple grounds, his minders
say it's his soul let loose, free and like a lemon moon, it glows.

Lord Ganesha monitors his Godliness – a deity with words
of wisdom, resplendent and holy in prayerful repose.

I long to touch his flap-wide ears, flick the tassel on his tail,
stroke his stipple-grain skin and wash the dust off his toes.

Whistles at Varanasi Station

He's wearing a white dhoti, decked in beads
and flowers, red tikka on his forehead, he takes both
my hands and tells me he's a Brahmin soothsayer.

I tell him my nightmares about my manager,
he speaks of curses, of cures – of how I must mix
green snake blood with mustard seed and frogs' legs.

He recommends honey in tea before going to sleep,
presses his fingers across the routes of my palm
and says I'll be riding horses again in my new life.

He guarantees his recipes, blesses me with water
from the Ganges, and stares at my suitcase, father's
leather brown belt pulled tight round its middle.

In a Bedside Drawer
(for my father)

in a B & B by the sea,
I find a black-and-white Kodak photo
of a man wearing a tie,
his long trousers rolled up
and a beach in the background.
He's holding a little girl
high on his shoulders.
Their faces crowd my room.

The man reminds me of my father –
how he too would wear his tie
to the beach, his orange-red cricket club tie.
He carried me on his shoulders,
holding my hands in his hands
and whistling *It's a long way to Tipperary*
beating the air and stamping
his feet on the sand.

I've visions of my father
back home on leave from Africa,
on a drizzling, cold, summer night,
stirring my cup of chocolate,
adding extra hot milk and sugar
reading me a story from *Alice*
as I snuggled under satin-edged blankets,
warmed by a hottie.

The Call
(for Maj)

In summer months, she'd drive down south
with Auntie Edna in her Morris Minor, driving
on B-roads with sandwiches and flasks of tea.

She'd sit with grandchildren on her knee,
playing games with words in a Collins Graphic
English Dictionary – spelling out the impossible.

Lately, she wasn't well enough to visit and she
promised us she wouldn't paddle in the sea
or ride her bike – instead she stayed inside

listening to the radio – a stickler for no waste,
she pulverised left-overs and used stewed teabags
to feed her cuttings and plants in the porch.

She made collages out of broken china, dried
fish bones and poppy heads. She hoarded tea,
tins of spam and long life milk, just in case.

I suppose we shouldn't have been surprised,
a shrill voice saying: Are *you next of kin*?
Mumblings of names and details. We kept

repeating Arrow Park as we raced up north.
All I could think of was, she wouldn't want a fuss.
I hoped they'd turned her lights off.

When I Tell You She Loved *Hello Dolly*

You have to understand it was mother-in-law's
favourite. I see her in her 30's silk dressing gown,
dancing in her lounge in her first floor flat,
blonde-grey hair up in a soft bun, wisps loose,
cheeks flushed like a girl – bars on an electric fire
switched on, red lights behind fake coal, a glass
cabinet displaying her Clarice Cliff tea-set.

When I tell you we asked the hotel waiters
to sing a surprise on her eightieth, sing *Hello Dolly*,
you have to imagine how they turned the lights off
as they carried in the cake with eighty candles
and her kissing the waiters on their cheeks, dividing
up the ice-cream sponge, the band playing *her* song,
a lady in a spin, a slice for everyone.

She asked us to play *Alfie* at her funeral.
We did, knowing the song said so much about her,
about her thoughts on life, its meanings.
We asked the minister to let us play *Hello Dolly*
at the end, hoping that everyone would leave
the church thinking about her in ways of laughter,
tapping their feet, and singing words to *her* song.

Keeping Going
(for Paul)

We've decided to lessen the work in our garden,
convert a striped lawn into a wildflower meadow.
It's speckled with clover, buttercups, lady's slippers
and daisies. Here Emily and Katie free woodlice
and spiders from the homemade sandpit built
with planks from a wooden floor. In the holidays,
they paint pictures on easels wearing Bumpy's
worn-out shirts, taking turns to sit on a rusty swing
covered in ivy. We barbecue on a home-made grill perched
on red slabs of an ancient coal bunker and eat sausages
on a seat that was once great-granny Margaret's bedhead.
Inside, we've kept more than we should – mother's
1940s frocks and furs hanging in our cupboards beside
her red make-up box with powder puffs and lipsticks.

The Shopkeeper

Her shop is propped up by clothes pegs; its floor of towels spreads out in a crook on the landing. Miri aged six wears a fringed gold evening stole over her long dark hair, a silver lurex skirt and a pink chiffon top. She's put on drop pearl earrings and a glitter bead necklace. She covers the carpet floor with scarves perfumed with breezes of ghosts, scents of Apple Blossom, English Lavender, Lily of the Valley and White Fire. She writes an inventory in her note book – counting paper pound notes, taking stock of the piles of lace hankies, coral beads, pearl pendants, ruby and emerald glass antique brooches and bracelets of all shapes and sizes. Jamie, aged three, wears bangles and a red-dotted handkerchief knotted on the side of his head – he sits on the bottom of the stairs piling up old pennies, shillings and sixpences. And when the shopkeeper opens up, she sells her young customer earrings, hankies and gloves through the gaps in the banisters. He pays with his great-grandma's money saved up in her silver-clip blue leather purse.

The Artist

I've painted watercolour washes
over a black-blue sky, streaks of crimson
spread from a crack on the horizon
of a restless, endless ocean.

I've veined in rivulets on a pale
summer moon, inked in the intricate
splinters of saffron glass
in the eye of a caged eagle.

I've mixed cadmium pale yellow
with cerulean for the inside tone
of a portrait in oils of Violetta,
and her husband Fernandez.

I've used acrylic windsor lemon
and cobalt violet on the petals
of an iris, mixed prussian blue
with chartreuse green for the stalk.

But it's the girl I met in Waitrose
with tinted glasses and a white stick
I want to sketch, her air of something
I could neither touch nor know.

The Man in the Kiosk

I've lost sight of the man on platform 4
who every weekday morning poured
Earl Grey tea into my cardboard cup.

He knew my name, often admired
my Welsh wool cape, winked at me
when I wore bright pink lipstick.

When there were leaves on the line,
or a body on the track, he wrapped
a Danish pastry in a paper napkin,

ignoring the queue, its whispers.
Then one day he was gone. I'd lost
a sun lark, a lilted accent, gone

was the smile that tracked his face
back to a home town in Sierra Leone.
Gone were the stories of his brothers

and his mother Claudetta who sewed
pleated frocks for school-girls and sang
in the hill-town choir of Segbwema.

I've lost sight of the man on platform 4
who every weekday morning poured
Earl Grey tea into my cardboard cup.

Epsom Derby Day

Glamour fashion girls slip by in short frocks
and fancy hats with feathers and flowers.
Gypsies pin bunches of purple heather on
collars, jackets and handbag straps. Young
men in waist-coats and ties talk on mobiles
to tipsters. People picnicking on the Downs
place bets with bookies shouting the odds.
TV screens fill an afternoon sky showing
previous winners like Shergar & Nijinsky.
Jockeys in caps and matching silks parade
their horses in a paddock. Four-leaf clovers
& blessed medals hidden under the saddles.

Horses canter to the start line, the white flag
drops – a hunch of hooves explode from metal
cages and the commentator gallops in non-stop
chat... *the favourite's lagging;* then name after
name, number after number, as riders race
towards Tattenham Corner. The crowds on
the hill shrieking and waving *C'mon! C'mon!*
The final post and a camera flashes the winner.
At the end, tipsy punters stroll to the station,
top hats tilted, the girls walking in stockings,
carrying their shoes. The Queen passes by in
a Rolls, winning fivers hidden in her handbag.

Waterloo Road

He walked into the supermarket in a gold-buttoned cassock,
a pellegrina and a brimmed black hat. He blessed me,

splashing holy water from a metal flask – *Deus benedicat!*
He blessed a lady pushing a trolley, blessed an old man

with a grey anorak, he knocked over a bottle of ketchup,
sent cans of beans tumbling. I could hear the manager's voice

repeating *unacceptable behaviour* – over and over again.
He'd gone before we had any time to shout in his defence.

I wish I'd spilt coffee beans all over the clean white floor.
The girl on the till says he's a patient, thinks he's a prophet,

that he speaks Italian and Urdu and changes outfits to suit
his mood. She likes his bright Maharaja's garments best.

Aunt Joyce

She never lost her Englishness living a life
in other lands – insisting on tea in a china cup
and linen napkins for Sunday lunch.
I told her wild tales of strawberries growing
on blossom trees and how English girls
still blushed at the sight of a naked oak.
We'd play Scrabble in the Italian mid-day sun
in made-up Aunt Joyce language – me fumbling
on a slick slack word, she laughing as she
pencilled in her points, never missing a trick.
After she died, I missed her ocean long calls
in the middle of a night, our marmalade talks
of orange peel and cats – a corner of my world,
where we shared our history and our art.

Willow

You're like *The Angel of the North*, the way you
own the heavens, your arms sweep across
an empty pale grey sky. I love your light, the way
you startle air, shape gaps, and sway towards
the sun. You know the hurt of rain, the tenderness
of water. In twilight you're a vision to behold,
a gilded icon as the sun slips behind you coppering
your edges. You're a healer of the sick – the juice
from your sap, your bark soothes my headaches.
If I sleep with a wand made from your wood
I'll dream of a pink moon and hear Celtic music
playing on harps. I love you clothed in catkins,
dressed in summer's leaves, bare in the winter.
Most of all I love the way you look at me.

Loose Thoughts

I'm dreaming of waterlily streams; flocks
of swallows wake me up as they leave behind
fields of hollow nests. I'm told they've clocks
inside their hearts – time ticking, time to remind
these white bellied, red throat blue backs to fly
long distances searching warmth across rough seas
towards the Sahara; forked tails in an open sky
winging ways over and through the Pyrenees.

Our thoughts inside ourselves are beyond us,
as strange as silence sounds, as strange as fear,
they float away like clouds passing – no fuss.
At times we live beyond our minds, disappear
in folds of darkness – long nights woken by light,
an early morning sun, a song-bird in flight.

It's the Way

they greet you; welcome you to most places,
flocks waiting: Somali, Swahili, Arabian-golden,

Parrot-billed, Yellow spotted, Yellow-throated.
Sparrows – all with an outer feather, extra

tongue bone, triple pecks picking up crumbs,
bits dropping on balconies of high-rise flats.

It's the way they puddle-dip, heads under water,
wings splashing backwards, frills of wet feathers.

I talk to them in low whispers, they're on my table,
laugh as one dips deep into my white milk jug.

I promise more cake as friends fly in, dive in,
help themselves – whirls of bird-skirts, sharp chirps.

It's the way they know where the lonely are,
by scattered seed on ledges, a wooden seat in the park.

Prize Day Antic

Sitting, squared solid in a crowded
tent, I glimpsed a tiny ant, alone
and lost on one huge mass
of a stranger's jacket. And despite
the herds of togethered parents,
he seemed to me quite unique.
And so I watched this ant manoeuvre
pranks dancing on the brown
worn weave and felt a sort of pride
at this small creature present
amidst the prize-borne day
and long hot speeches. Then this
minute being staged for me
his cunning dance: turning, twirling,
groping like a man lost in strange surrounds.
He sent a sort of irritation,
a skin-fluffed needle, enough to receive
one hasty-hot enquiring hand
upon the pink-fleshed playground of a neck.
And still he pranced
and feathered thorns.
And to this day, I don't suppose
that father knows,
one tiny ant shared with me the glitter
of the prizes and disappeared
in the darkness of his neck.

Phone-in

'I can't believe he does it,
he knows he never should
and it's in the shed Doctor, in the shed,
and I never knew Doctor, I never knew
and I can't believe he's been
doing it all those years Doctor,
all those years...

And it's the deceit Doctor,
the deceit. He has a new
electric wheelchair Doctor,
a new electric wheelchair...
because for six long years
I was pushing him Doctor,
six long years...

He's living on borrowed time Doctor,
living on borrowed time, time he
doesn't deserve Doctor.
It's my time too Doctor, my time too
and my nerves are bad Doctor,
my nerves are bad,

He's eighty-two Doctor,
eighty-two and after all those
operations he's deceived me, deceived me.
After all I've done, all I've done
and the worst is my friends knew
my friends knew... and no-one told me Doctor,
no-one told me... I've just found out...
He's been smoking Doctor,
he's been smoking...'

Every Saturday

we waited at the bus-stop, girls in boots, miniskirts,
black-bitty curled-up mascara eyelashes, bee-hive
brushed hair, ticked eyes and white-pink lipstick.

Swanky boys wolf-whistled at us, their arms winging
sideways, hanging on to a metal pole on the jump on,
jump off platform of the bus – the conductress clipped

our tickets from a wind-up machine on a leather strap
round her neck, tinging the bell twice at the Odeon stop.
Inside we queued under a chandelier's broken shades

handing our money to a man smoking alone in a kiosk,
his yellow stained fingers counting up our change.
In the hall, posters of past movies stared down at us.

The Pink Panther, Breakfast at Tiffany's – we were shown
in to the cinema by an usherette in a frilly hat and apron,
her silver torch poking holes in the dark, quietly and,

with a no 'hanky-panky' look in her eye, she pointed
to the back row, our seats with ashtrays on the corners
lit by a shaft of light from a projector beaming down.

We sat in silence admiring the gold velour fringed drapes
on either side of the stage in the red velvet auditorium.
A lion's head roaring – turning – ready to swallow us up.

The Man in the Art Gallery Guarding the Room
with Medieval Artwork

I was supposed to be analysing and appreciating
the intricacies of the artist Bellini, his wondrous
medieval masterpieces with so much detail. You
looked so lonely sitting on your chair in the corner
of the room with your name badge hung low on
your chest. I know you're supposed to be keeping
an eye open in case someone tries to do a runner
or damage one of the paintings. I was worried about
the woman in the green coat, she had an open bag
and pushed past me in a strange way – I was trying
to read the comments written about the self-portrait
of the artist, you didn't seem to notice us – you
looked as though you were asleep. Somehow, I
think you're different, your aquiline nose, thick
grey-brown hair in a pony tail and hands with long
fingers make me think that perhaps you're an oil
painter in your spare time, perhaps you're an out
of work actor, or perhaps you're an ex con. I prefer
people watching and guessing who they are rather
than taking too long looking at the exhibition. Once
in another gallery I asked someone else in a role like
yours what he thought about all day. He laughed as
he said he mostly thought about timings for his breaks.

.

Another Elvis

He was born with a slipping hip that meant he could wiggle in a way that only orthopaedic academics really understood. They wrote a paper about his condition in the *New England Journal of Medicine* – they used anthropological methodology.

He had a passion for buying fresh flowers, on account of his beloved grandmother Anna Theresa who owned a florist shop in a town called Dancing Horses, he lived with her as a child. She taught him to speak conversational French and Cantonese.

He was colour-blind and thought when he wore red, he was wearing silver-blue, it was hard to select snazzy outfits for performances; the many popular songs that he wrote in French made reference to tribulations – *Je suis tourmenté.*

He adored his sister, his wife and was proud of all the kids though some thought it was ridiculous that they named his first child January. He was addicted to puzzles and enjoyed equations in algebra with philosophical arguments in Latin.

He had a hang-up about his teeth falling out, wore snoozes, mouth-guards filled with glue-like paste that looked like snow. His father gave him a life-time subscription to a motorbike magazine – he was an insomniac and avid reader of T.S. Eliot.

Benches on the Prom

he fed sea birds here

still they squat beside his seat, peck air, stare
sideways, wish his orange quilted anorak
would reappear, that he'd throw crusts again

if you are here I am with you

two men in black brimmed hats sit side by side
most days they save a space
eat sandwiches on their laps, drink tea in flasks

once more unto the beach

friends crowd this bench, wearing velvet coats
high boots, they speak in actors' voices, drink
bubbly, take it in turn to recite his lines

smoke me a kipper, I'll be back for breakfast

some nights he sleeps here, wrapped in a brown
duffle coat, smokes roll-ups same as his old pal
dips a digestive in his flask of coffee

I'll see ya on the ice kid

he tracks her skates, sees her diamante skirt
his binoculars focussed on skit-skat clouds
she's dancing, dancing backwards

War Zone

Shocked, limbs aching, part mute – swearing in
local lingo, the wounded limp in bandaged feet.
Close by, their silenced comrades lie in long neat
rows swaddled as babes, their names fixed by a pin.
At dusk an old man is seen holding an open jar
flamed by a candle, stooping as he counts the dead.
His son is missing. The land is filled with lead
bullets, metal from heavy gun blasts. Bodies are
hidden in dust-filled ditches in the sweltering heat.
Here shadows act as ghosts beneath a bombed street
where no birds dare to land – this landscape is new,
yellow ochre skies with marigold lips, a city pensive,
torn apart… a soldier mutters, he's dreaming of blue
skies, he's back home rinsing strawberries in a sieve.

Notes Talking to Each Other

(Skaragos Camp outside Athens)

most days a mother weeps
inside herself, the waves turn over
curl under her

her daughter in a scrap of shade
sits in the corner of the camp
practising the guitar, children

in flip-flops and baggy leggings
clap their hands
plead for another tune

on Thursdays a music teacher instructs
the boys and girls how to play Mozart
on flutes, clarinets, violins

young musicians from Iraq, Syria
and Afghanistan share music stands
play together for the missing

the mother, as she listens,
wipes her tears and opens up
her white-gold palms

4th March 2014

today in the Crimea
Russian marksmen
fired gun shots

into an unowned sky
against unarmed
Ukrainian soldiers

history speaks
of unspeakable atrocities
of uninvited armies

my untracked family
from Lwów
shot by Stalin's bullets

no named patch of grass
to kiss the ground
touch their names

no headstones
to place bunches of white
scented roses

today I thought I saw
my mother in the crowds
waving to the boys

on the boundaries
calling them back
in Polish

Personal Acknowledgements:

These poems are collected from many years of writing. Thanks to all my tutors especially Roger McGough, Roddy Lumsden, and Mimi Khalvati. Anne-Marie Fyfe for inspiration on her courses, Coffee-House Poetry events and workshops at the Troubadour; Gillian Clarke, Carol Ann Duffy, Maura Dooley for courses at Ty Newydd, and Sue Burge for mentoring me; to my poet friends in the Lambs poetry group, the Roddy Lumsden group, to Elizabeth Rumbelow who directed the Poetry & Music Ensemble that I founded in 1984 and who encouraged my writing; to the Poetry School for so many great courses and latterly the online courses; to The Poetry Society for ongoing inspiration; to my colleagues on the Arts Forum for their support and the Royal Marsden NHS Foundation Trust who have given me the title of Artist in Residence. The royalties from this book will go to The Royal Marsden Cancer Charity. I am grateful to my brother, Oliver, for arranging a visit back to Zambia after many years. Thanks to my sister, Nicky, for her support; to my friend Mumba Sheyo for her help with Bemba translations; Jean Hall and Paul Stephenson for their great encouragement over the years; to Mimi, Paul, Sue and Jean for advice on poems in this manuscript; to Ronnie Goodyer and Dawn Bauling, editors of Indigo Dreams, for their patience with me and for making this book possible. Finally, thanks to my wonderfully supportive husband, Paul, to my children, Mike and Debs, and their families, all of whom have cheered me on with the many poetry projects I've been involved in and continue to enjoy.

Previous Publications & References

Some of these poems, or versions of them, have appeared in anthologies and magazines including: The Interpreter's House, Weyfarers, Magma, Poetry Space, Artemis Poetry, Poem, N2 Poetry, Sentinel Literary Quarterly, The Hippocrates Book of the Heart, Fanfare. 'Prize Day Antic' was highly commended by Alan Brownjohn in the Wayfarers Competition 1986. 'War Zone (Front Line) highly commended in Paragram Competition 2014. 'It's Near (I'm listening to forecasts of violent winds)' and The Lady in The Isle of Mull (The Shepherd) are two of five poems shortlisted for the 2014 Flambard Poetry Prize.' Lion in Chingola' was a second prize winner in the Sentinel 2015 competition. 'The Artist (Sight Beyond)' was commended in the Sentinel 2016 competition. 'The Call' was commended in the 2017 Sentinel competition. 'Threads' was a prize-winning poem in the 2016 Troubadour International Poetry Competition. 'Watching the Boys, My Freckles Burning' was long-listed in the 2016 National Poetry Competition. 'Every Saturday' prize winner in the Film Competition 2016. 'An Award Winning Care Home (Too Far)' was highly commended in the Creative Writing competition for Carers UK in 2017. 'In the Fifties' was a third prize winner in the 2017 Robert Graves Competition. Several poems commended in the 2017 Gregory O'Donoghue International Poetry Competition. Many of the poems in the book were short-listed in the Indigo First Collection Competition 2018. 'The Man in the Kiosk (Platform 4)' and 'After Sacro Monti di Ossuccio' were set to music by the composer Lucas Jordan, performed in Switzerland and the UK. Thanks to Hattie Garlic for permission to write 'Notes talking to each other' from The Times June 2018 I've used titles of various songs: 'Hello Dolly 'was written by Jerry Herman 1964. 'Alfie' was written by Burt Bacharach in 1966. 'It's a long way to Tipperary' written in 1912 by Jack Judge & Harry Williams. 'The Angel of the North' – a sculpture by Antony Gormley in 1998 in Gateshead.

Indigo Dreams Publishing Ltd
24, Forest Houses
Cookworthy Moor
Halwill
Beaworthy
Devon
EX21 5UU
www.indigodreams.co.uk